# PRIDE

## The Story of Harvey Milk
## and the Rainbow Flag

Written by

Rob Sanders

Illustrated by

Steven Salerno

Random House 🏠 New York

*In memory of my uncle Jack Sanders*
*—R.S.*

Visit us on the Web! randomhousekids.com

Educators and librarians, for a variety of teaching tools,
visit us at RHTeachersLibrarians.com

*Library of Congress Cataloging-in-Publication Data*
Names: Sanders, Rob, author. | Salerno, Steven, illustrator.
Title: Pride : the story of Harvey Milk and the Rainbow Flag / by Rob Sanders ;
illustrated by Steven Salerno.
Description: First edition. | New York : Random House, [2018]
Identifiers: LCCN 2016046632 (print) | LCCN 2017003025 (ebook) |
ISBN 978-0-399-55531-2 (hc) | ISBN 978-0-399-55532-9 (glb) |
ISBN 978-0-399-55533-6 (ebk)
Subjects: LCSH: Milk, Harvey—Juvenile literature. |
Gay politicians—California—San Francisco—Biography—Juvenile literature. |
Gay pride celebrations—California—San Francisco—Juvenile literature. |
Gay liberation movement—United States—Juvenile literature. |
Gay rights—United States—History—Juvenile literature.
Classification: LCC F869.S353 M54569 2018 (print) | LCC F869.S353 (ebook) |
DDC 979.4/61092 [B]—dc23

Book design by Nicole de las Heras

MANUFACTURED IN CHINA
10 9 8 7 6 5 4 3
First Edition

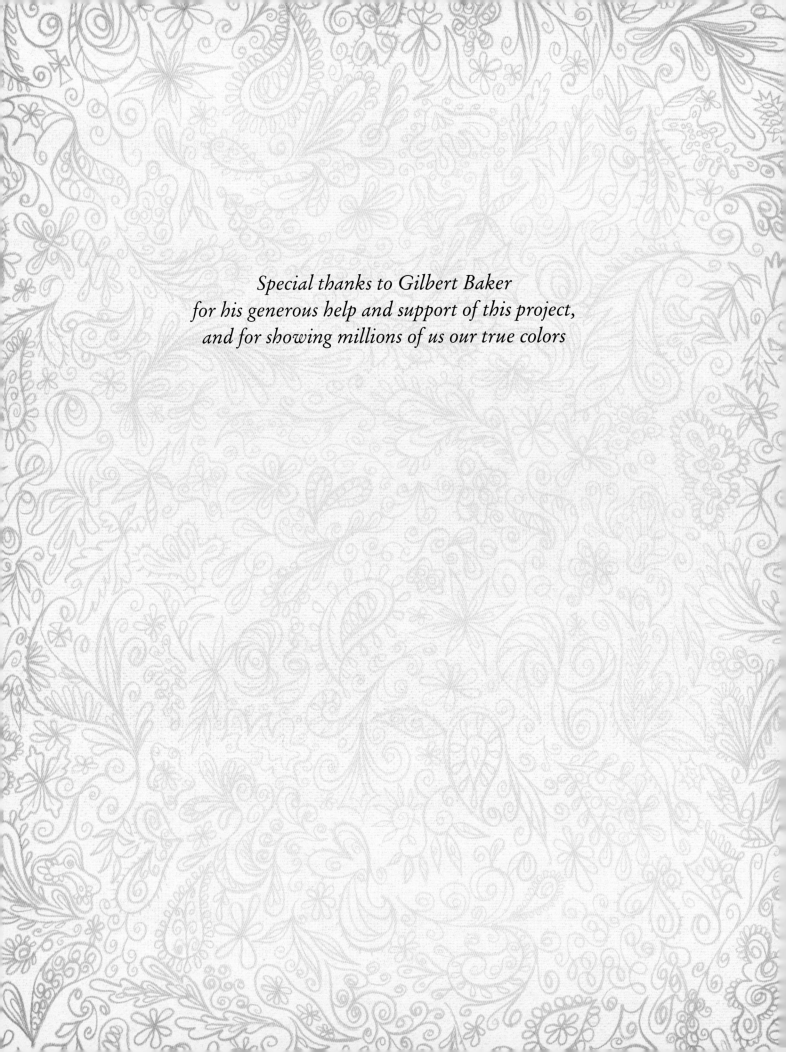

*Special thanks to Gilbert Baker*
*for his generous help and support of this project,*
*and for showing millions of us our true colors*

"You have to give them hope.
Hope for a better world, hope for a better tomorrow. . . ."

Harvey Milk was an ordinary man, but he had an extraordinary dream.
That dream would change history.

Harvey dreamed that everyone—even gay people—would have equality.

He dreamed that he and his friends would be treated like everyone else.

He dreamed that one day, people would be able to live and love as they pleased.

With his New York accent, Harvey talked to everyone about his dream.

His voice boomed. His body bounced with energy and excitement.

STRAIGHTS
FOR
GAYS

I LOVE MY
GAY SON

PASS GAY RIGHTS BILL

GAY

GAYS MUST GO

GOD
SAYS
NO

Some people listened.
A few agreed.
Most did not.

But Harvey's big voice and his big dream wouldn't be stopped. He discovered that the best way to *change* laws was to help *make* laws.

In 1977, Harvey Milk took a big step toward that dream when he became one of the first openly gay people to be elected to political office in the United States.

Harvey and his friends planned marches to protest inequality and unfair laws.

And just days before one of the marches, Harvey had an idea.

*A symbol,* he thought. *We need a symbol that shows who we are and how we feel.*

Something to carry during the march. Something to make
people feel they're part of a community.
Something to give people hope. Something extraordinary.

Harvey knew an artist who could help—Gilbert Baker.
Harvey asked.
Gilbert said, "We need a flag!"

Volunteers arrived to help Gilbert's design come to life.
Together they dipped fabric into large barrels filled with
vivid, vibrant dyes.
They cut and pieced and sewed until . . .

. . . Harvey, Gilbert, and the other activists had a flag.
A flag with eight colorful stripes.
A flag that Harvey hoped would give hope.

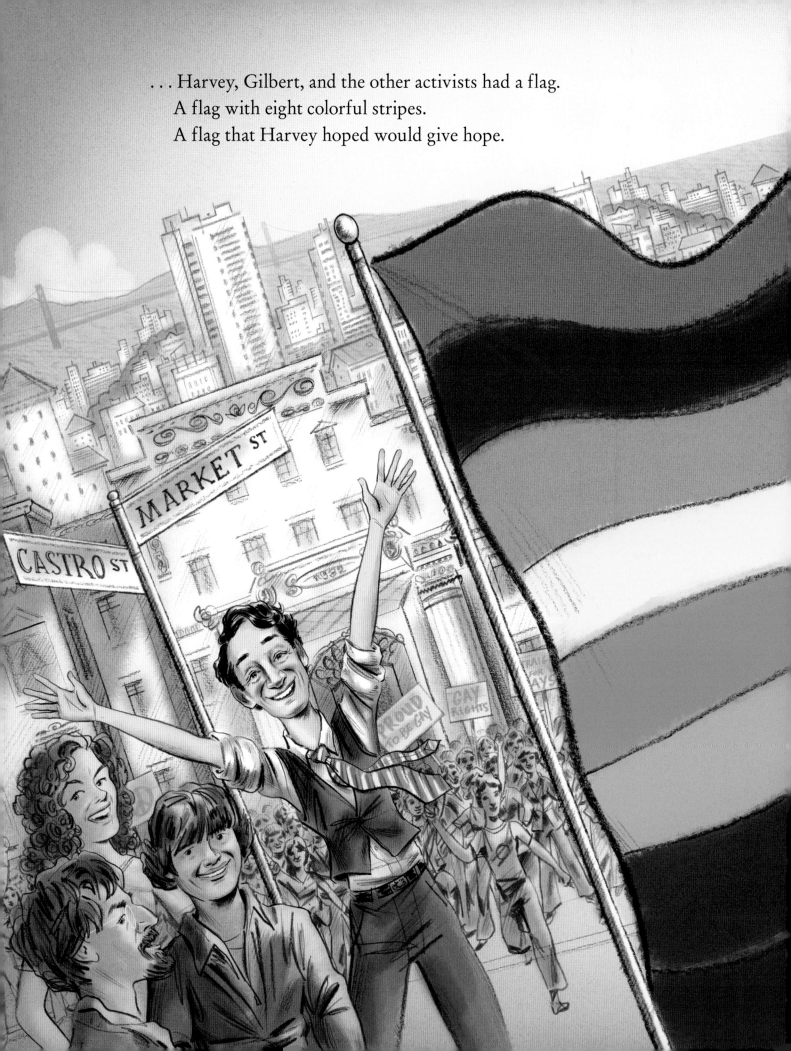

"Rights are won only by those who make their voices heard."

On June 25, 1978, when it was time for the march,
a breeze stirred in San Francisco.
The flag unfurled.

The wind blew.
The flag fluttered, flapped, and flew.
A rainbow, as bright and unique as the men and women
who walked behind it, led the march.

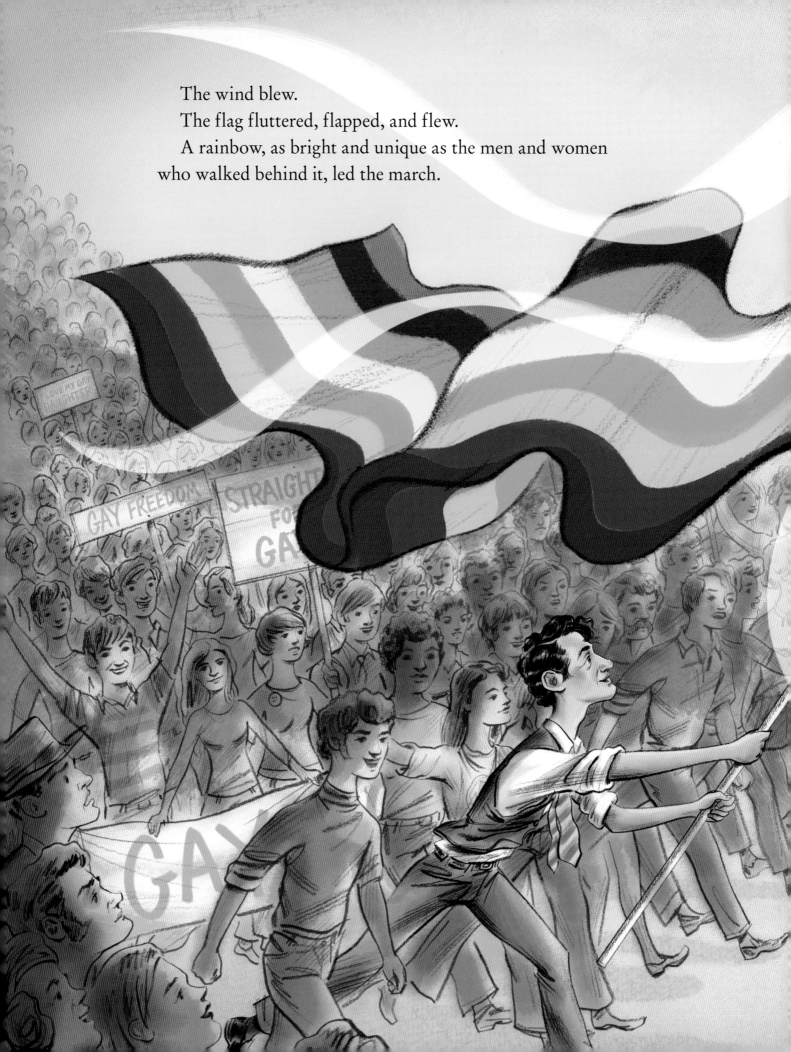

Harvey and the people asked for equality.
They asked to be treated like everyone else.
They asked to live and love as they pleased.
They hoped the march would make a difference.

Harvey was proud of the flag, and proud of himself.

He hoped others could be proud, too.

The flag did not fly on that dark, sad night.

Instead, thousands and thousands of people marched silently, carrying candles.

The candlelight wove through the streets of San Francisco, up and down hills and around city buildings.

A mile of glowing candlelight in honor of two lives lost.

That could have been the end of Harvey's dream and the colorful flag.

But it wasn't.

More Rainbow Flags were created.
Some of the colors changed. Eight stripes became six stripes.
But the meaning of the flag did not change.
It was a flag of equality.
More and more people began to think of the flag as their flag.
And they began to feel pride.
They began to have hope.

In 1994, Gilbert Baker designed another Rainbow Flag. This one was larger than all the rest.

Women and men, side by side, carried the flag: a proud, mile-long rainbow floating through New York City. The flag wove through the streets, up and down avenues and boulevards and around city buildings.

The people demanded equality.

They demanded to be treated like everyone else.

They demanded to live and love as they pleased.

They were proud. They had hope. They would make a difference.

More Rainbow Flags were made.
Some were printed on bumper stickers and T-shirts.
Others were hoisted onto lampposts on Halsted Street in Chicago.
One was hung in the Museum of Modern Art in New York City.
Soon, the Rainbow Flag was flying in other countries, like Brazil,
England, Israel, Russia, Singapore, and Turkey.

The Rainbow Flag now unfurled on farms, in suburbs, and in cities.

The flag flew proudly outside public buildings, hotels, shops, restaurants, churches, and homes.

And once, on June 26, 2015, the White House was awash
in the colors of the Rainbow Flag.

Equality.
Pride.
Hope.
Love.

Harvey's dream
became a flag for us all.

# BIOGRAPHICAL NOTES

The Rainbow Flag is also known as the Pride Flag. For decades, an upside-down pink triangle was the only symbol associated with homosexuals. Adolf Hitler introduced the triangle to shame gay men, and to identify them when they were sent to concentration camps. Harvey Milk realized that the gay and lesbian community needed a new, positive symbol, and the Rainbow Flag was born. The original flag, designed and created by Gilbert Baker and a group of volunteers, had eight stripes. From top to bottom, they were: hot pink, red, orange, yellow, green, turquoise, indigo/blue, and violet. The Rainbow Flag now includes red, orange, yellow, green, royal blue, and violet.

Harvey Milk was born in Woodmere, New York, on May 22, 1930. He studied math and history at New York State College for Teachers. He served in the navy, taught public school, and worked as a production associate on Broadway. He moved to San Francisco in 1972 and opened a camera shop. When he won a seat on the San Francisco Board of Supervisors in 1977, Harvey Milk became one of the country's first openly gay people elected to public office. He asked Gilbert Baker to create a symbol to carry in a gay-rights march he was organizing, and Gilbert created the Rainbow Flag. Harvey Milk was assassinated, along with Mayor George Moscone, by Dan White on November 27, 1978, just months after the first Rainbow Flag was flown.

Gilbert Baker was born in Chanute, Kansas, in 1951. His grandmother owned a men's clothing store, and he wanted to learn to sew because he loved fabrics. As an adult, Gilbert joined the army, and he eventually moved to San Francisco. Once he was settled in his new home, he bought a sewing machine. Harvey Milk asked him to create a symbol for the gay community, and that was when Gilbert designed the Rainbow Flag. He went on to design many other banners, flags, and works of art. Gilbert continued to be a gay-rights activist until his death on March 31, 2017.

June 26, 2015, was historic. On that day, the Supreme Court of the United States of America ruled that gays and lesbians have a constitutional right to marry. They are free to live and love as they please.

# HARVEY MILK—A TIME LINE

**May 22, 1930**
Harvey Bernard Milk is born in Woodmere, New York.

1947
Graduates from high school.

1951
Graduates from New York State College for Teachers with a degree in mathematics.

1951–1955
Serves in the U.S. Navy. He is a deep-sea diver on the U.S.S. *Kittiwake*.

1957–1961
Works as a high school math and history teacher and basketball coach.

**1963–1970**
Works in New York as a public school teacher, a stock analyst, and a Broadway production associate.

**June 28, 1969**
Beginning of Stonewall riots for gay rights in Greenwich Village, New York City.

1973
Harvey opens the Castro Camera shop in San Francisco.

1974
Forms the Castro Village Association and organizes the first Castro Street Fair to help attract people to local businesses.

1976
Appointed to the Board of Permit Appeals by Mayor George Moscone.

**November 8, 1977**
Elected to the San Francisco Board of Supervisors. This is his fourth run for office and his first win.

**January 9, 1978**
Inaugurated in San Francisco's City Hall.

**April 1978**
Mayor George Moscone signs a San Francisco gay civil rights ordinance, which Harvey introduced, making it illegal to discriminate against someone because they are gay.

**June 25, 1978**
Harvey rides in the Gay Freedom Day Parade. The first Rainbow Flag flies in the parade.

November 27, 1978
Harvey Milk and Mayor George Moscone are assassinated by former city supervisor Dan White.

# THE RAINBOW FLAG—A TIME LINE

**1978**
Harvey Milk has the idea for a flag to represent the fight for equal rights for gay men and women.

Gilbert Baker creates the flag with about thirty volunteers, who dye and sew together two versions. The flag has eight stripes at first, but as the years go on, it will only have six.

**June 25, 1978**
The flag makes its first appearance in the Gay Freedom Day Parade in San Francisco. Harvey rides in the parade.

**1979**
Gilbert Baker arranges for the Paramount Flag Company to mass-produce the flag. Hot pink is removed from it, and indigo is changed to royal blue.

The San Francisco Gay Freedom Day Parade committee decides to use the new flag in its parade to honor Harvey. The committee wants an even number of stripes, so turquoise is removed.

**1994**
Ten thousand people carry a thirty-foot-wide, mile-long Rainbow Flag through Manhattan during New York City's Pride celebration. *The Guinness Book of Records* confirms that it is the world's largest flag.

**2004**
Gilbert Baker unveils a re-creation of the eight-striped flag during the Key West Pride Festival in Florida.

**June 26, 2015**
The Supreme Court rules that gay couples have the right to get married. The White House and other buildings across the United States are lit with the colors of the Rainbow Flag.

# ≡ FOR FURTHER READING ≡

## WEBSITES

milkfoundation.org

nyclgbtsites.org

queerkidstuff.com

San Francisco Public Library, LGBTQIA Archives
(sfpl.org/index.php?pg=2000003701)

## BOOKS

*Gay & Lesbian History for Kids: The Century-Long Struggle for LGBT Rights*
by Jerome Pohlen

*I Am Jazz*
by Jessica Herthel and Jazz Jennings

*Pride: Celebrating Diversity and Community*
by Robin Stevenson

## PODCAST
*Making Gay History*